THE EVERYTHING®

Christmas
RECIPES

MINI BOOK

D1072992

Adams Media Corporation
Avon, Massachusetts

An Everything® Series Book.
"Everything" is a registered trademark of Adams Media Corporation.

Published by Adams Media Corporation
57 Littlefield Street, Avon, MA 02322
www.adamsmedia.com

ISBN: 1-58062-544-4

Printed in Canada.

J I H G F E D C B A

Library of Congress Cataloging-in-Publication Data
available from the publisher.

Many of the designations used by manufacturers and sellers to distinguish their
products are claimed as trademarks. Where those designations appear in this
book and Adams Media was aware of a trademark claim, the designations have
been printed in initial capital letters.

This publication is designed to provide accurate and authoritative information with
regard to the subject matter covered. It is sold with the understanding that the
publisher is not engaged in rendering legal, accounting, or other professional
advice. If legal advice or other expert assistance is required, the services of a
competent professional person should be sought.
      — From a *Declaration of Principles* jointly adopted by a Committee of the
American Bar Association and a Committee of Publishers and Associations

Cover illustrations by Barry Littmann.
Interior illustrations by Barry Littmann, Kathie Kelleher, and Susan Gaber.

This book is available at quantity discounts for bulk purchases.
For information, call 1-800-872-5627.

Visit the entire Everything® series at everything.com

Table of Contents

CHAPTER 1

Breakfasts, Brunches, and Breads

Applesauce Loaf

½ cup butter, softened

1 cup granulated sugar

1 large egg, room temperature

1½ cups all-purpose flour

1½ teaspoons baking soda

1 teaspoon ground cinnamon

¾ teaspoon nutmeg

½ teaspoon salt

½ teaspoon ground cloves

1½ cups unsweetened applesauce

½ cup dark raisins

½ cup coarsely chopped walnuts

confectioners' sugar

1. Preheat oven to 350°F. Grease and flour a 9" × 5" loaf pan.

2. In a medium bowl, cream butter and sugar together until light and fluffy. Beat in the egg.

3. In another bowl, mix together flour, baking soda, cinnamon, nutmeg, salt, and cloves. Gradually beat flour mixture into butter mixture.

4. Beat in applesauce.

5. Stir in raisins and nuts.

6. Pour batter into prepared pan.

7. Bake loaf for 1 hour, or until a toothpick inserted into the center comes out clean. Transfer pan to wire rack. Cool for 10 minutes. Remove loaf from pan and cool completely.

8. Dust with confectioners' sugar.

Baked French Toast with Whipped Cream and Strawberries

2 large eggs

1/4 cup milk

1 teaspoon vanilla extract

6 slices day old white bread

3 tablespoons butter

2 tablespoons granulated sugar

1/2 teaspoon cinnamon

1 cup heavy cream, whipped,
 or 1 pint vanilla ice cream

3 cups sliced, sweetened strawberries

1. Preheat oven to 400°F.
2. In a medium bowl, beat eggs, milk, and vanilla.
3. Place bread in a shallow dish. Pour egg mixture over bread and let stand for 5 minutes, then turn bread over once with a rubber spatula and let stand for 5 minutes more.
4. Melt butter in a 13" × 9" × 2" baking pan in oven for 5 minutes.
5. When bread has absorbed egg mixture, transfer bread to baking dish. Sprinkle with cinnamon and sugar and bake approximately 25 minutes, or until well browned and puffy.
6. Serve with whipped cream and strawberries.

Cranberry Bread

2 cups all-purpose flour

1 cup granulated sugar

1½ teaspoons baking powder

½ teaspoon baking soda

1 teaspoon salt

¼ cup shortening

½ cup orange juice

1 teaspoon grated orange peel

1 large egg, lightly beaten

½ cup chopped walnuts

1 cup frozen cranberries,
   chopped into halves

1. Preheat oven to 350°F. Grease a 9" × 5" loaf pan.

2. Sift together flour, sugar, baking powder, baking soda, and salt.

3. Using a pastry blender or 2 knives held together, cut in shortening until coarse crumbs form.

4. In a separate bowl, combine orange juice, orange peel, and egg.

5. Make a well in the center of the dry ingredients. Add egg mixture all at once to the well, tossing with a fork until just moistened.

6. Stir in the nuts and cranberries. Spread batter in prepared pan. Bake until a toothpick inserted in the center comes out clean, approximately 1 hour.

7. Remove bread from pan; cool completely.

Christmas Morning Biscuits

Yield: 12 biscuits

2 cups flour

1 tablespoon baking powder

$^1/_2$ teaspoon salt

1 tablespoon sugar

$^1/_3$ cup butter or shortening

$^3/_4$ cup milk

1. Preheat oven to 425°F.
2. Sift together the flour, baking powder, and salt. Stir in the sugar.
3. Cut the butter or shortening into the dry ingredients until the mixture resembles coarse crumbs.
4. Add the milk all at once, and mix quickly with a fork just until a dough forms.

5. Turn onto a floured board and knead gently about 10 times. Roll or pat the dough to a ³/₄-inch thickness and cut with a biscuit cutter or 2¹/₂-inch round cutter.

6. Place on an ungreased cookie sheet and bake 12 to 15 minutes, or until golden brown.

Variations on Christmas Morning biscuits:

Buttermilk Biscuits: Add ¹/₄ teaspoon baking soda and omit sugar. Substitute buttermilk for whole milk.

Drop Biscuits: Increase milk to 1 cup. Combine ingredients well, but do not knead. Drop by tablespoon onto a greased cookie sheet.

Christmas Morning Waffles

2 cups sifted cake flour
4 teaspoons baking powder
¼ teaspoon salt
2 large eggs
1¼ cup plus 1 tablespoon milk
6 tablespoons vegetable oil or melted butter

1. Grease and preheat an electric waffle iron.
2. Sift together the dry ingredients.
3. Beat the eggs with an electric mixer.
4. Add milk and dry ingredients alternately until just blended.
5. Stir in oil or melted butter.
6. Spoon batter onto prepared waffle iron and cook until golden brown and crisp. (Cooking times will vary.)

Eggs à la Buckingham

5 large eggs, lightly beaten
$\frac{1}{2}$ cup milk
$\frac{1}{2}$ teaspoon salt
$\frac{1}{3}$ teaspoon pepper
5 slices toasted white bread
1 tablespoon butter
grated Cheddar cheese to taste

1. Preheat oven to 350°F.
2. Arrange toast slices in a baking dish.
3. In a large bowl, combine eggs, milk, salt, and pepper.
4. Melt butter in skillet; cook eggs until just scrambled. (They should appear slightly undercooked.)
5. Spoon eggs over toast; sprinkle with desired amount of grated Cheddar cheese.
6. Bake until cheese melts, approximately 5 minutes.
7. Serve immediately.

Elfin Popovers

Yield: 6 popovers

1 cup flour
½ teaspoon salt
2 eggs
1 cup milk
1 tablespoon melted shortening or oil

1. Preheat oven to 475°F. Grease well a popover pan or six 6-ounce custard cups.
2. Sift together the flour and salt.
3. In a separate bowl, beat the eggs well, and add the milk to them.
4. Add the flour mixture, and beat with an electric mixer on medium speed for 1 minute.
5. Add the melted shortening and beat 1 minute more.

6. Fill the prepared cups half full. Bake at 475°F for 15 minutes, then reduce heat to 350°F and continue baking 25 to 30 minutes longer, until well browned.

7. A few minutes before they are to be removed from the oven, carefully prick each popover with a fork to allow steam to escape. Remove immediately from the pans.

Note: Bake alone in the oven for best results. Serve immediately and hot!

Fancy Nancy's Christmas Irish Bundt Bread

3 cups all-purpose flour

3 teaspoons baking powder

$^3/_4$ cup granulated sugar

$1^1/_2$ cups milk

$^1/_3$ cup vegetable oil

1 egg

1 cup golden raisins, tightly packed

1 tablespoon caraway seeds

Icing:

1 cup confectioners' sugar, sifted

$1^1/_2$ tablespoons hot water or milk

$^1/_2$ teaspoon vanilla flavoring

Green or red food coloring

1. Preheat oven to 350°F. Grease and flour a
   9" bundt pan.
2. In food processor, combine flour, baking powder,
   and sugar and process.
3. In a large bowl, mix together milk, oil, and egg.
4. Pour the liquid mixture into food processor
   with the flour mixture; pulse until blended
   and smooth.
5. Pour mixture back into mixing bowl. Add raisins
   and seeds. Mix well.
6. Pour batter into prepared pan.
7. Bake bread until a toothpick inserted into the
   center comes out clean, approximately 35–45
   minutes. Cool for 25 minutes in the pan.
   Cool for 1 hour on a rack.
8. Mix icing ingredients together and drizzle
   over bread.

German Coffee Cake

1 cup margarine, softened
2 cups granulated sugar
4 large eggs, at room temperature
1 pint sour cream
2 teaspoons vanilla extract
2 teaspoons baking soda
1½ cups all-purpose flour
3 teaspoons baking powder
½ cup chopped walnuts

Topping:

½ cup granulated sugar and 2 teaspoons cinnamon,
   mixed together in a small bowl

1. Preheat oven to 350°F. Grease a 9" × 13" baking pan.
2. In a large mixing bowl, cream together margarine and sugar.
3. Add eggs, sour cream, baking soda, and vanilla.
4. Beat in flour and baking powder. Stir in walnuts.
5. Pour half of the batter into baking pan.
6. Sprinkle half of the topping over batter; run a knife once through batter to distribute topping.
7. Pour remaining batter into the pan; then run a knife once through batter.
8. Bake until a toothpick inserted into the center comes out clean, approximately 40–45 minutes.
9. Transfer baking pan onto a wire rack. Cool for 30 minutes.

Holiday Lemon Nut Bread

2½ cups all-purpose flour

1 cup granulated sugar

3½ teaspoons baking powder

½ teaspoon baking soda

½ teaspoon salt

½ teaspoon grated lemon peel

½ cup water

⅓ cup shortening, melted

2 large eggs, lightly beaten

½ cup fresh lemon juice

1 cup chopped walnuts

   (or ½ cup nuts and ½ cup raisins)

1. Preheat oven to 350°F. Grease and flour a 9" × 5" × 3" loaf pan.
2. In a large bowl, sift together flour, sugar, baking powder, baking soda, lemon peel, and salt.
3. Combine water, shortening, eggs, and juice. Make a well in the center of the dry ingredients. Pour egg mixture into the well, tossing with a fork until dry ingredients are just moistened. Stir in nuts and/or raisins.
4. Spread batter into prepared pan.
5. Bake bread until a toothpick inserted into the center comes out clean, approximately 60–75 minutes.
6. Let cool for 10 minutes; remove from pan. Cool on wire rack for 5 minutes. Wrap in plastic and refrigerate until ready to serve.

Rudolph's Raspberry Cream Cheese Breakfast Biscuits

Yield: 15 biscuits

3 cups flour

2 tablespoons baking powder

$3/4$ teaspoon salt

3 tablespoons shortening

$3/4$ cup orange juice or milk

1 package (3-ounce) cream cheese

2 tablespoons raspberry all-fruit spread or jam

1. Preheat oven to 450°F.
2. Sift together the flour, baking powder, and salt.
3. Cut in the shortening until the mixture resembles coarse crumbs. Add the orange juice and beat to form a soft dough.
4. Turn dough onto a surface well dusted with flour and knead 10 times.
5. Roll or pat the dough till it is ½-inch thick.
6. Cut rounds with a biscuit cutter or a 2½-inch round cutter (a drinking glass can be used). Place the rounds on an ungreased cookie sheet.
7. Soften the cream cheese. Add the jam and mix until marbled but not thoroughly combined.
8. Spoon about 1 teaspoon of the cheese mixture onto the center of each round. Sprinkle with sugar.
9. Bake 8–10 minutes, or until golden brown.

Note: You can replace the flour, baking powder, salt, and shortening by substituting 3 cups of prepared biscuit mix, such as Bisquick.

Santa's Jolly Scones

Yield: 12 scones

2¼ cups cake flour
1 tablespoon baking powder
½ teaspoon salt
2 tablespoons sugar
5 tablespoons butter
1 egg
½ cup light or heavy cream*

1. Preheat oven to 425°F.
2. Sift the flour, baking powder, salt, and sugar together.
3. Cut in the butter until the mixture is the size of small peas. Make a well in the mixture.
4. Beat the egg lightly and combine with the cream. Pour the liquids into the dry ingredient well, and combine quickly but thoroughly.

5. Turn onto a lightly floured work surface. Pat or roll the dough to a thickness of about $3/4$ inch. With a sharp knife, cut into diamond shapes.

6. Brush the tops with cream and sprinkle with sugar. Bake 12–15 minutes on an ungreased cookie sheet.

Variation: Add $1/2$ cup raisins or currants when adding the egg-cream mixture to the dry ingredients. Or use $1/3$ cup dried cherries or dried mixed fruits that have been steamed briefly to plump.

Note: If substituting all-purpose flour for the cake flour, reduce the amount to 2 cups and knead 10 times before shaping and cutting.

*Cream gives scones their characteristic richness; do not substitute milk.

Special Holiday Sausage Quiche

Yield: 2 single-crust pies

1 pound hot sausage
$^{1}/_{2}$ cup chopped onion
$^{1}/_{2}$ cup chopped green peppers
2 cups grated cheese
4 tablespoons flour
$^{1}/_{2}$ teaspoon salt
4 large eggs
1 can (8-ounce) evaporated milk
2 unbaked pie shells

1. Preheat oven to 350°F.
2. Sauté sausages, onion, and pepper in a skillet; remove from heat and drain well.
3. In a large bowl, mix cheese, flour, and salt.
4. In another bowl, beat together eggs and milk.
5. Combine all ingredients in the large bowl.
6. Divide mixture evenly between 2 unbaked pie shells.
7. Bake until top is golden and set, approximately 30–45 minutes.
8. Let cool for 10 minutes.

Very Merry Mocha Coffee Mix

16 ounces instant coffee

2 cups cocoa powder

4 teaspoons ground cinnamon

2 teaspoons ground nutmeg

water (amount will vary depending
on the number of cups you
are preparing)

1. In a mixing bowl, sift together dry ingredients.
2. Boil required amount of water in a kettle, then pour into medium-sized mugs.
3. Add one spoonful of mixture to each mug—or more or less, according to taste.

CHAPTER 2

Appetizers

Antipasto

1 pound American cheese, sliced
$^1\!/_2$ pound imported ham, sliced
$^1\!/_2$ pound imported Genoa salami, sliced
$^1\!/_2$ pound prosciutto, sliced
$^1\!/_2$ pound mortadella, sliced
1 can (12-ounce) tuna, packed in oil and
   undrained
1 full head lettuce
$^1\!/_2$ pound imported sharp provolone cheese, cut
   into 1-inch chunks
1 jar (8-ounce) pepperoncini
1 jar (8-ounce) green stuffed olives
olive oil
red wine vinegar

1. Roll slices of meat with American cheese and line along the outside of a large platter, alternating the different kinds of meat.
2. Wash, dry, and break up the lettuce and arrange in the center of the plate.
3. Spread tuna on top of lettuce, being sure not to drain any oil from the can.
4. Arrange provolone around the lettuce.
5. Top with olives and pepperoncini.

Dressing: Mix three parts olive oil to one part red wine vinegar. Serve separately.

Blitzen's Tomato Bruschetta

Servings: 8

8 slices French bread
2 cloves garlic, halved
1 teaspoon olive oil
2 tablespoons minced onion
1 diced tomato
pinch of oregano, crumbled
pinch of pepper
2 tablespoons grated Parmesan cheese

1. Toast the bread on both sides. Rub one side of each piece of toast with the cut side of the garlic. Keep hot.

2. Heat the oil in a nonstick skillet over medium-high heat. Add the onion and cook, stirring until tender, about 10 minutes.

3. Remove from the heat and stir in the tomato, oregano, and pepper.

4. Spoon the tomato mixture over garlic-rubbed side of the toast, dividing evenly. Sprinkle with the cheese and brown slightly under a preheated broiler for 1 minute. Serve immediately.

Christmas-Colored Stuffed Peppers

Servings: 6

6 large squat green and red peppers

$\frac{1}{2}$ cup converted (parboiled) long-grain rice

$\frac{1}{2}$ cup water

$\frac{1}{2}$ pound ground beef

$\frac{1}{4}$ cup diced celery

$\frac{1}{4}$ cup chopped onion

1 can (16-ounce) diced tomatoes

salt and pepper

1 can (8-ounce) tomato sauce

1. Preheat oven to 350°F.
2. Slice off the tops of the peppers and clean and seed the insides.
3. Bring a large kettle of water to a boil and blanch the peppers for about 5 minutes. Remove and invert to drain.
4. In a small saucepan, bring the rice and $\frac{1}{2}$ cup water to a boil; cover and simmer for 5 to 10 minutes, or until water is absorbed.
5. In a large bowl, mix the beef, celery, onion, and rice. Stir in the tomatoes, and salt and pepper to taste. Fill the peppers, mounding the filling on top if there is enough.
6. Place upright in a deep-sided baking dish; peppers may be touching. Pour the tomato sauce over the peppers.
7. Cover and bake 1 hour; uncover and bake an additional 15 minutes. Filling may remain somewhat pink even when well done.

Christmas Eve Artichoke Dip

Servings: 4

2 cans (15-ounce) artichoke hearts, drained and
   rinsed

1 red pepper, finely chopped

1 green pepper, finely chopped

3 cloves garlic, minced

2 cups of mayonnaise

white pepper

2 wedges Parmesan cheese (approximately
   1 pound), grated

1. Preheat the oven to 325°F. Mix all ingredients
   except $1/4$ of the Parmesan cheese.

2. Place the mixture in a 9" × 9" baking pan or
   $1^1/2$-quart casserole dish and sprinkle remaining
   Parmesan cheese over the top.

3. Bake for 45 minutes, or until golden brown.
   Serve with crackers or bread.

Christmas Fondue

1 cup butter
1 cup all-purpose flour
4 cups milk
2 cups Chablis
2 teaspoons chicken flavored bouillon powder
Cheddar cheese, thinly sliced, about 1½ pounds

1. Melt the butter in a large saucepan. Stir in the flour; cook for several minutes over low heat.
2. Add the milk, Chablis, and bouillon powder; stir frequently until mixture thickens.
3. Stir in cheese until melted and smooth. (Use more or less cheese, according to your own taste.)
4. Transfer to a fondue pot; keep warm.
5. Serve with slices of bread and raw vegetables.

Christmas Nacho Crisps

¹/₂ cup yellow cornmeal
¹/₂ teaspoon salt
1³/₄ cups boiling water
1 teaspoon margarine

1. Preheat oven to 425°F. Grease a baking sheet.
2. Mix cornmeal and salt in a bowl. Mix in 1 cup of boiling water. Blend.
3. Add margarine, stirring until melted; add remaining water; stir.
4. Drop mixture by rounded teaspoonful (drop should be a little bigger than a quarter) onto prepared baking sheet.
5. Bake nachos until golden and crisp, 12–15 minutes, or until golden brown.
6. Serve with salsa.

Christmas Party Mix

2¹/₂ tablespoons Worcestershire sauce

16 cups rice and corn cereals of your choice
   (Chex, for instance), evenly combined

1¹/₂ cups small pretzel sticks

3 cups salted peanuts

2 teaspoons salt

1¹/₂ cups margarine, melted

1. Preheat oven to 275°F.
2. Combine all the ingredients except the butter.
3. Drizzle melted butter over cereal mixture, stirring
   to distribute it evenly.
4. Bake in shallow pan for about an hour,
   stirring occasionally; check often during the
   last 15 minutes to be sure mixture does not
   overcook.

Holiday Shrimp Dip

3 cans small deveined shrimp, drained
2 packages (8-ounce) cream cheese, softened
1 bottle (12-ounce) shrimp sauce
crackers of your choice
parsley

1. Combine shrimp and cream cheese.
2. Add 1/2 bottle shrimp sauce and mix well.
   Place mixture in a mold of appropriate size,
   and chill overnight.
3. Invert mold onto a platter. Spoon remaining
   sauce over top as if frosting.
4. Garnish with parsley and serve
   with crackers.

Mrs. Claus's Special Spinach Dip

Servings: 6

1 package (10-ounce) frozen spinach, thawed
2 cups sour cream
1 cup mayonnaise
1 envelope vegetable soup mix (Knorr brand)
1 small white onion, chopped
1 can (8-ounce) water chestnuts, drained
   and chopped
2 tablespoons grated Parmesan cheese

1. Squeeze out water from thawed spinach and
   do not cook. Add all other ingredients and mix.
2. Serve with raw vegetables, crackers, or a
   sourdough bread loaf that has been hollowed
   out and cut into bite-sized pieces.
3. Spinach dip can be served inside the round
   hollowed out loaf of sourdough bread.

Reindeer Crunches

1 envelope onion soup mix
1 cup butter or margarine, softened
12 slices white bread, crusts removed

1. Preheat oven to 350°F.
2. Blend soup mix with butter.
3. Spread onion soup mixture on each slice.
4. Cut each slice into four strips.
5. Place bread slices on a baking sheet. Bake until golden brown, approximately 10 minutes.

Rick-Dimi-Ditty

1 tablespoon of butter or margarine
1/4 medium-sized onion, finely chopped
1 can condensed tomato soup
1/2 pound American cheese, sliced fine
1 egg
1 teaspoon Worcestershire sauce
salt to taste
crushed red pepper flakes to taste

1. In a large saucepan, melt butter; stir in onion.
2. Add soup with 1/2 can of water.
3. Bring the soup to a boil, stirring often.
4. Stir in the cheese. Mix well. Lower heat.
5. In a small mixing bowl, beat the egg,
   Worcestershire sauce, salt, and pepper flakes.
   Stir egg mixture into saucepan. Stir constantly.
6. Cook until mixture thickens. Do not boil.
7. Serve with crackers of your choice.

Stuffed Mushrooms

Servings: 6

1 pound of mushrooms
   (caps approximately 1½-inches across)
3 tablespoons butter
½ cup onion, finely chopped
¾ cup bread crumbs
½ teaspoon salt
freshly ground pepper to taste
1 teaspoon dried thyme
¼ cup cream (or half and half)
¼ cup finely grated Parmesan cheese
2 tablespoons chopped parsley

1. Preheat oven broiler.
2. Clean the mushrooms and gently pull the stem from each cap, setting the caps aside.
3. Chop the mushroom stems and set aside. Heat butter in a skillet over medium heat. Add the onion and cook for 1 minute.
4. Add the chopped mushroom stems and cook for an additional 2 to 3 minutes.
5. Stir in the bread crumbs, salt, pepper, and thyme, and continue to cook for 1 minute more. Remove from heat and stir in cream and grated cheese.
6. Using a small spoon, fill each mushroom cap with the mushroom mixture. Place the filled mushrooms on a baking sheet and put under the preheated oven broiler for 5 to 7 minutes, or until the tops are browned and caps have softened and are slightly juicy.
7. Sprinkle the tops with chopped parsley and serve hot or warm.

Swiss Fondue

Servings: 6

1 clove garlic, halved
2½ tablespoons flour
1 cup vegetable broth
⅔ cup evaorated milk
½ teaspoon brandy extract
2 ounces Swiss cheese, shredded
2 tablesoons grated Parmesan cheese
3 ounces cream cheese, cubed
⅛ teaspoon freshly ground pepper
⅛ teaspoon ground nutmeg
1 loaf crusty French bread, cubed

1. Rub the inside of a fondue pot or saucepan with cut sides of the garlic. Discard the garlic.
2. Whisk the flour and $1/4$ cup of the broth in a measuring cup until blended.
3. Add the remaining broth and milk to the pot, and heat over low heat until very hot but not boiling.
4. Whisk in the extract and the flour mixture. Cook, stirring constantly, 2 to 6 minutes.
5. Stir in the Swiss, Parmesan, and cream cheeses, pepper, and nutmeg. Cook, stirring constanly, until the cheeses melt and the mixture is very smooth.
6. If you don't have a fondue pot, transfer to a Crock-Pot or casserole with a warming unit. Serve with bread cubes.

CHAPTER 3

*Side Dishes
and Soups*

Cheesy Cauliflower with White Sauce

2 (2-pound) cauliflower heads, trimmed

water

juice of 1 lemon

salt

1 bay leaf

4 tablespoons butter

3 tablespoons flour

2 cups cool milk

2 small onions, peeled, studded with cloves

1 1/2 cups shredded Cheddar cheese

1. Pour water into a large bowl. Soak cleaned, washed, and stemmed cauliflower head-down in cold water for about 10–15 minutes. (Water should cover cauliflower.)

2. Drain, then break cauliflower into florets. Steam, partially covered, in a saucepan with lemon juice, salt, and bay leaf.

3. Cook until tender, about 10–12 minutes.

4. While cauliflower cooks, melt butter over low heat in a saucepan. Stir in flour and cook for approximately 4 minutes, stirring constantly.

5. Pour in milk. Mix well.

6. Add the onions. Beat until smooth and glossy.

7. Remove from heat. Add in cheese, stirring until melted and smooth.

8. Place cauliflower florets on a serving dish. Cover florets with sauce. Serve immediately.

Christmas Pumpkin Soup

4 cups chicken broth

8 cups canned pumpkin purée

5 cups milk, scalded

6 tablespoons firmly packed brown sugar

6 tablespoons butter

1½ cups boiled ham, finely diced

salt to taste

parsley

dash of nutmeg

1. In a large pot, mix broth and pumpkin until smooth.

2. Stir in milk. (If you prefer creamier soup, add more milk.)

3. Stir butter, brown sugar, ham, and salt into pumpkin mixture.

4. Heat soup until it simmers. Garnish with parsley and nutmeg.

Dasher's and Dancer's Vinaigrette Dressing

Yield: ¾ cup

¼ cup red wine vinegar
1 tablespoon fresh lemon juice
1 teaspoon prepared Dijon mustard
salt and freshly ground pepper to taste
½ cup extra-virgin olive oil

1. Mix together the vinegar, lemon juice, mustard, salt, and pepper.
2. Add the olive oil a little at a time, beating with a whisk until the mixture emulsifies.
3. This dressing can also be made in a blender. Mix all the ingredients and blend at high speed for a very short time.

Elves' Own Sautéed Broccoli and Sweet Peppers

Servings: 4

1 pound broccoli
1 tablespoon olive oil
2 teaspoons unsalted butter
$1/2$ each red and yellow bell pepper, julienned
2 cloves garlic, minced
salt and pepper

1. Cut broccoli into bite-sized florets and blanch in boiling water until tender, about 2–3 minutes. Shock in ice water to preserve color, and drain. Set aside.
2. Heat oil and butter in a sauté pan or skillet over medium-high heat. Sauté peppers for 3 minutes.
3. Add broccoli and garlic. Sauté until thoroughly heated and lightly browned, about 3–4 minutes.
4. Season with salt and pepper to taste.

Frozen Cranberry Salad

1 cup heavy cream
1 cup crushed pineapple, drained
1 can whole or jellied cranberry sauce
2 tablespoons mayonnaise
2 tablespoons granulated sugar
2 packages (8-ounce) cream cheese, softened
¾ cup walnuts, coarsely chopped

1. Whip cream in a large mixing bowl.
2. Stir pineapple into whipped cream. Set aside.
3. In a blender or food processor, process cranberry sauce until smooth.
4. Add mayonnaise, sugar, and cream cheese, and continue to process until well blended. Stir in nuts.
5. Fold cranberry mixture into whipped cream. Pour into molding tray of your choice; cover and freeze.
6. Let salad stand at room temperature for 15 minutes before serving. Slice and serve on lettuce.

Glazed Onions

Servings: 6–8

18 medium white or yellow onions
4 teaspoons sugar
1 teaspoon dry mustard
$^{1}/_{2}$ teaspoon salt
6 tablespoons butter, melted
$^{1}/_{4}$ teaspoon paprika

1. Preheat oven to 325°F.
2. Peel onions and simmer whole in water for 15 minutes.
3. Drain the onions and arrange in a shallow baking dish.
4. Combine sugar, mustard, salt, and butter; pour over onions.
5. Sprinkle with paprika and bake for 20 minutes, or until tender when pierced with a sharp knife.

Glazed Turnips or Rutabagas

Servings: 4

2 pounds turnips or rutabagas
2 tablespoons butter
¼ cup honey
¼ teaspoon ground ginger
salt and freshly ground pepper to taste

1. Peel turnips or rutabagas and cut into 1/2- inch thick, quarter-sized slices.
2. In a pot of boiling water, cook turnips for 8 minutes, rutabagas for 15 minutes, or just until tender.
3. Drain. Stir in butter and cook over high heat, shaking pan often, until vegetables are coated with butter.
4. Stir in honey, ginger, and salt and pepper. Cook, stirring often, for 1 minute, or until glazed. Serve immediately.

Green-and-Red Stuffed Tomato Treat

Servings: 6

2 heads fresh broccoli

3 teaspoons butter or margarine

3 large ripe tomatoes

4 ounces shredded Fontina cheese

¼ teaspoon ground nutmeg

¼ cup heavy cream

1 teaspoon salt

⅛ teaspoon pepper

Note: Depending on the sizes you select, you may
need more broccoli or tomatoes; buy extra to be
on the safe side.

1. Preheat oven to 350°F.
2. Grease a large baking dish.
3. Cut off broccoli florets. In a large saucepan, steam them until tender, 5–10 minutes. Drain broccoli. In a blender or food processor, process broccoli until smooth.
4. In a large saucepan, melt the butter. Add the broccoli; cook over medium heat for about 3 minutes, or until broccoli is tender.
5. Add cheese, nutmeg, cream, salt, and pepper. Cook, stirring frequently, until cheese melts. Do not overcook. Set the mixture aside.
6. Slice tomatoes horizontally. Remove seeds and pulp with a spoon, leaving a small indentation.
7. Spoon the broccoli mixture evenly into the center of each tomato half.
8. Place the tomatoes in prepared baking dish.
9. Bake for 8–10 minutes, or until tomatoes are tender.

Mexican Christmas Eve Salad

fresh lettuce

2 medium apples, peeled, cored, and
   thinly sliced (about 2 cups)

1 medium banana, sliced

lemon juice, fresh or bottled

1 cup navel orange sections (about 2 oranges)

2 cups pineapple chunks, drained

1 can (1-pound) sliced beets, drained

½ cup unsalted peanuts

½ cup pomegranate seeds

nondairy whipped topping

1. Line a large serving platter with lettuce leaves.
2. In a large bowl, mix sliced apples and bananas.
   Sprinkle with a little lemon juice
   (it keeps them from turning brown).
3. Arrange apples, bananas, orange sections,
   pineapple chunks, and beets over the lettuce.
4. Sprinkle peanuts and pomegranate seeds
   over fruit.
5. Serve whipped topping on the side; each
   guest may use more or less dressing according
   to taste.

Night Before Christmas Leek and Potato Soup

Servings: 8

4 large leeks

2 tablespoons butter

2 potatoes, peeled and cubed

1 onion, chopped

4 cups chicken stock

1 cup milk

salt and pepper

2 tablespoons light cream

$^1/_4$ cup chopped fresh chives

1. Trim the outer leaves and dark green tops from the leeks. Cut lengthwise in half almost all the way through, leaving the root end intact. Spread the leaves and rinse in cold water. Shake off the water and chop leeks to make about 4 cups.

2. In a large, heavy saucepan, melt the butter over low heat. Add the leeks, potatoes, and onion. Cover and cook, stirring occasionally, for 15 minutes, or until softened.

3. Add the stock and simmer gently, covered, for about 20 minutes, or until the vegetables are tender.

4. In a blender or food processor, purée the soup, in batches if necessary, until smooth.

5. Return to the saucepan. Add the milk and heat through. Season with salt and pepper to taste.

6. Serve hot or chilled, garnished with a swirl of cream and a sprinkle of chives.

No-Turtle Soup

¼ teaspoon butter
1¼ cups diced veal cutlets
2 packages powdered onion soup mix
water
sour cream
dried parsley

1. In a large saucepan, melt butter.
2. Sauté veal (which is similar in taste to turtle meat) lightly over low heat, approximately 10 minutes. Be sure to cook meat thoroughly. Remove from heat and set aside.
3. Prepare onion soup according to package directions.
4. While soup is hot, drain off solids and discard them.
5. Add cooked veal to prepared broth.
6. Garnish with dollops of cold sour cream sprinkled with parsley. Serve immediately.

Reindeer's Favorite Belgian Carrots

Servings: 4

2 pounds fresh carrots, thinly sliced

½ cup butter

1 teaspoon salt

⅓ cup fresh chopped parsley

2 bunches fresh green onions, chopped

1. Preheat oven to 350°F.
2. Place sliced carrots in a 2-quart baking dish. Set aside.
3. Sauté butter, salt, parsley, and green onions in a saucepan over medium heat for 5 minutes, or until onions become slightly translucent.
4. Pour mixture over carrots, stirring slightly.
5. Bake for 50 minutes, or until carrots are tender. Serve immediately.

Santa's Salad Niçoise

Servings: 4 main-dish servings

3 medium potatoes (approximately 1 pound)

8 ounces fresh green beans, trimmed (or 9-ounce
package frozen cut green beans, thawed)

½ cup cucumber, pared and diced

¼ cup sliced black olives

1 can (7-ounce) white tuna, drained and flaked

⅔ cup Dasher's and Dancer's Vinaigrette Dressing
(page 57) or oil-and-vinegar "French-style"
dressing

lettuce leaves, optional

2 ripe tomatoes, cut into wedges

2 hard-boiled eggs, sliced

1. Pare and dice the potatoes; boil and steam them until tender.
2. Cook or steam green beans until barely tender.
3. In a bowl, layer the green beans, cucumbers, olives, tuna, and potatoes. Drizzle the dressing over the top. Cover and refrigerate until well chilled.
4. When ready to serve, toss the salad. Arrange on lettuce leaves, if desired, and top each serving with tomato wedges and egg slices.

Slow-cooked French Onion Soup

Servings: 6

4 large yellow onions, thinly sliced

$1/4$ cup butter

3 cups rich beef stock

1 cup dry white wine

1/4 cup medium dry sherry

1 teaspoon Worcestershire sauce

1 clove garlic, minced

6 slices of French bread, buttered

$1/4$ cup grated Romano or Parmesan cheese

1. In a large frying pan, slowly sauté the onions in butter until transluscent and glazed. Transfer to the Crock-Pot.

2. Add the beef stock, white wine, sherry, garlic, and Worcestershire sauce. Cover. Cook on low-heat 6 to 8 hours.

3. Preheat the boiler. Place the buttered French bread on a baking sheet. Spinkle with cheese. Place under the broiler until ightly toasted.

4. To serve, laddle the soup into 6 bowls. Float a slice of toasted French bread on top of each serving.

Southern California Yorkshire Pudding

$1/4$ cup pan drippings reserved from roast beef

6 large eggs

2 cups milk

$1\frac{1}{2}$ teaspoons salt

$1\frac{1}{2}$ teaspoons Worcestershire sauce

$1\frac{1}{2}$ cups all-purpose flour

$2\frac{1}{2}$ cups cooked and cooled wild rice

1. Preheat oven to 450°F.
2. Pour 1 teaspoon of the pan drippings into each of 12 muffin-pan cups. Place muffin pan in preheated oven for 2–3 minutes.
3. Blend eggs, milk, salt, and Worcestershire sauce in a large bowl. Mix well. Add flour, stirring until blended.
4. Add rice. Pour batter evenly into the hot drippings in prepared pan.
5. Bake until brown and puffy, approximately 25 minutes.

Southern Style Christmas Corn

1 can chopped corn (whole kernels), drained
2 large eggs, slightly beaten
1 teaspoon salt
$\frac{1}{8}$ teaspoon pepper
$1\frac{1}{2}$ teaspoons melted butter
1 pint scalded milk

1. Grease a large microwave-safe dish.
2. Mix corn, eggs, salt, and pepper.
3. Stir in butter and milk.
4. Pour corn mixture into prepared dish.
5. Microwave on high in 3-minute sessions for 10–15 minutes or until firm. (Note: Cooking times may vary dramatically by oven.)
6. Rotate and check frequently; do not overcook!

Special Green-and-Red Vegetable Salad

trimmed florets from 1 head broccoli

trimmed florets from 1 head cauliflower

1 pound carrots, sliced thin

1 pound fresh mushrooms, sliced into thin segments

1 medium green bell pepper, sliced into strips

1 medium red bell pepper, sliced into strips

2 small zucchini, sliced

4 stalks celery, sliced1 teaspoon tarragon leaves

Marinade:

¹/₄ cup vegetable oil

¹/₄ cup olive oil

1¹/₂ cups tarragon vinegar

2 large cloves garlic, minced

1¹/₂ teaspoons prepared mustard

¹/₄ cup granulated sugar

1¹/₂ teaspoons salt

1. Place vegetables in large salad bowl.
2. Combine all marinade ingredients. Mix well, and pour over vegetables. Toss well.

Spicy Herb Salad

Servings: 4

5 handfuls romaine leaves, chopped into
   bite-sized pieces
1 handful loosely packed whole mint leaves
$1/4$ cup whole green basil leaves
$1/2$ cup whole oregano leaves
$1/4$ cup finely chopped green onions
salt to taste

Vinaigrette:

$1/4$ cup olive oil
2 teaspoons red wine vinegar
2 tablespoons water
$1/2$ teaspoon salt
1 teaspoon Dijon mustard

1. Just before serving, combine the romaine with the mint, basil, oregano, and green onions in a large bowl. Lightly salt, and gently toss to mix well.

2. In a jar with a lid, mix the oil, vinegar, water, salt, and mustard. Shake well until all ingredients are completely blended.

3. Drizzle half the vinaigrette over the salad and gently toss to mix well. Add more vinaigrette if necessary.

Sweet Potato Soufflé

¹/₄ cup butter

¹/₄ cup all-purpose flour

1¹/₂ cups half and half

5 large eggs (room temperature), separated

¹/₄ cup grated Cheddar cheese

3 cloves garlic, crushed

1¹/₂ teaspoons salt

¹/₄ teaspoon pepper

¹/₄ teaspoon cream of tartar

1¹/₂ cups cold mashed sweet potatoes

1. Preheat oven to 375°F.
2. Grease a 2-quart soufflé dish with a collar extending 3 inches above the rim.
3. Melt butter in a large saucepan. Mix in flour and cook, stirring constantly, for 1 minute. Blend in the half and half; cook over low heat, stirring constantly.
4. Stir in egg yolks, 1 at a time. Stir in cheese, garlic, salt, and pepper, beating well after each addition.
5. Stir mashed potatoes into the egg mixture, and set aside.
6. In a large bowl, beat the egg whites with cream of tartar until stiff peaks form. Fold egg whites into the potato mixture.
7. Pour potato mixture into prepared dish.
8. Bake soufflé until the top is puffy and golden, approximately 50 minutes. Serve immediately.

Tiny Tim's Twice Baked Potatoes

Servings: 4 to 6

4 potatoes

1 tablespoon butter

2 tablespoons chopped onion

$\frac{1}{3}$ cup sour cream

up to $\frac{1}{4}$ cup milk

2 strips bacon, cooked crisp and crumbled
   (optional)

$\frac{1}{3}$ cup shredded Cheddar cheese

salt and pepper to taste

1. Preheat oven to 350°F.
2. Bake the potatoes and allow them to cool until they can be handled.
3. Meanwhile, melt the butter in a small skillet and cook the onion until softened, about 3 minutes.
4. Cut the potatoes in half lengthwise and scoop out the flesh, being careful to leave a shell of $\frac{1}{4}$ to $\frac{1}{2}$ inch.
5. In a medium bowl, combine the potato, sour cream, onion, and butter. Mash them together thoroughly, then beat by hand or with an electric mixer, adding as much milk as necessary for a smooth consistency. Potato mixture will be slightly firmer than mashed potatoes.
6. Add the bacon and cheese to the potato mixture, and season with salt and pepper to taste.
7. Mound the mixture in the potato shells. Place them on an ungreased baking sheet. Bake for about 30 minutes (or microwave on high for about 10 minutes), until well heated.

Wonderful Winter Baked Mashed Squash

Servings: 4

2¹/₂–3 pounds winter squash
5 tablespoons butter, divided
salt and freshly ground pepper to taste
brown sugar
¹/₄–¹/₃ cup chopped pecans
sour cream for garnish

1. Preheat the oven to 350°F.
2. Peel squash and steam or bake until tender. Mash.
3. Add 4 tablespoons butter to the squash and season to taste with salt and pepper.
4. Place squash in a buttered 1-quart baking dish, dot with remaining butter, and cover with a sprinkling of brown sugar and pecans.
5. Bake for 30 minutes. Garnish with sour cream.

Yorkshire Pudding

1 cup milk

2 large eggs

1 cup all-purpose flour

$^1/_4$ teaspoon salt

$^1/_2$ cup beef drippings from a roast (quantity may vary, depending on size of pan you use)

1. Preheat oven to 350°F.
2. Combine milk and eggs until well blended.
3. In a large mixing bowl, mix flour and salt. Add milk mixture into flour mixture so that it forms a smooth paste.
4. Cover bottom of hot pan with beef drippings.
5. Pour batter over drippings.
6. Bake pudding until golden, approximately 20 minutes.

CHAPTER 4

*Main Courses
and
Accompaniments*

Bread Crumb Stuffing

1⅓ tablespoon butter, melted
3 cups seasoned bread crumbs
¾ teaspoon salt
1⅓ tablespoons dried parsley
½ teaspoon pepper
8 drops onion juice
1 large egg, beaten well

1. In a large mixing bowl, drizzle butter over bread crumbs. Toss together with a fork.
2. Stir in salt, pepper, parsley, and onion juice, and mix well.
3. Mix in beaten egg.
4. Stuff poultry just prior to cooking. (You may wish to enlarge the quantities in this recipe if you are cooking a particularly large bird.)

Chestnut Poultry and Game Stuffing

4 cups French chestnuts
1¼ cups ground cracker crumbs
¾ cup butter
⅓ cup heavy cream
1¼ teaspoons salt
¼ teaspoon pepper

1. Shell the chestnuts.
2. Place chestnuts in enough boiling salted water to cover; cook until softened. (Cooking time will depend on size of chestnuts.) Drain, and coarsely mash the chestnuts.
3. Fold cracker crumbs, butter, cream, salt, and pepper into chestnut purée.
4. Stuff poultry just prior to cooking. (You may wish to enlarge the quantities in the recipe if you are cooking a particularly large bird.)

Christmas Almond Burgers

Servings: 6

4 pounds ground beef

½ pound finely ground blanched almonds

2 teaspoons salt

1 teaspoon pepper

¼ cup butter

1 small red bell pepper, cut into thin strips

1 small green bell pepper, cut into thin strips

1. Preheat oven to 400°F.

2. Fold almonds, salt, and pepper into the ground meat. Shape meat mixture into six large burger patties.

3. Place patties in a shallow pan and bake for 10 minutes.

4. Place a pat of butter evenly on the top of each patty. Bake for 10 more minutes, or until done to taste.

5. In a saucepan, steam the pepper strips until tender, and use them as a garnish for the meat patties.

Christmas Sweet and Sour Meatballs

1 pound ground beef, chicken, or turkey

1 cup seasoned bread crumbs

1 large egg, lightly beaten

2 tablespoons chopped onion

2 tablespoons milk

$^3/_4$ teaspoon salt

2 tablespoons solid vegetable shortening

1 can ($8^1/_4$-ounce) pineapple chunks, drained
   (reserve the juice)

1 tablespoon cornstarch

$^1/_4$ cup cold water

1 can (8-ounce) whole or jellied cranberry sauce

half of a 12-ounce bottle barbecue sauce

$^1/_4$ teaspoon salt

$^1/_2$ medium green bell pepper, cut into strips

1. Mix ground meat, bread crumbs, egg, onion, milk, and salt in a large mixing bowl. Using a table-spoon, shape meat mixture into meatballs.
2. In a large skillet, cook meatballs until browned. Drain off grease.
3. In a medium bowl, combine shortening, pineapple chunks, cranberry sauce, barbecue sauce, and salt. Add this mixture to the skillet.
4. In small container, dissolve cornstarch in cold water, and stir it into the skillet. Add the pepper strips.
5. Cover skillet and simmer for 15–20 minutes, or until peppers are tender. Add reserved pineapple juice a little at a time, until mixture reaches desired consistency.

Elegant Veal Loaf

Servings: 4–5

1 pound ground veal

$\frac{1}{4}$ cup soft bread crumbs

$\frac{1}{8}$ teaspoon white pepper

$\frac{1}{4}$ cup fresh chopped parsley

1 egg

1 tablespoon butter

4 ounces Gorgonzola or blue cheese, crumbled

2 tablespoons chopped toasted walnuts

1 tablespoon snipped fresh chives

1. Preheat oven to 350°F. Lightly grease an 8" · 11" baking dish.
2. Mix together the veal, bread crumbs, pepper, and parsley.
3. Lightly beat the egg and combine with the veal mixture.
4. Shape into a loaf in the baking dish. Then press a well the entire length of the loaf, about two-thirds of the way to the bottom of the loaf.
5. Soften the butter and combine with the cheese, walnuts, and chives.
6. Spoon the mixture into the well in the loaf, ending within $1/2$ inch of each end. Reshape the veal over the cheese filling.
7. Bake 50 minutes, or until juices run clear.

Fancy Brie-Stuffed Chicken Breasts

Servings: 4

olive oil

1½ cups thinly sliced onion

2 cloves garlic, peeled and thinly sliced

⅔ cup dry white wine

2 ounces Brie cheese

½ teaspoon salt

¼ teaspoon pepper

4 half chicken breasts, bone in and skin on

1 tablespoon butter, melted

1. Preheat the oven to 375°F.
2. In a large skillet, heat about 1 teaspoon olive oil over medium heat. Add the onions and sauté about 3 minutes, until golden brown.

3. Add the sliced garlic and sauté an additional
   5 minutes. Stir in the wine and cook about
   5 minutes or until the wine is almost evaporated.

4. Remove the onion mixture to a bowl. Cut the
   Brie into small pieces (rind should be removed),
   and stir into the onion mixture along with the salt
   and pepper; allow to cool slightly.

5. Remove the bones (but not the skins) from
   the chicken breasts. Loosen the skin from the
   breasts by working your fingers between the skin
   and the meat and gently separating them; leave
   the skin attached around 3 edges. Stuff a quarter
   of the onion-Brie mixture under the skin of
   each breast.

6. Place the chicken in a greased square baking pan,
   skin side up, and drizzle with the butter. Bake
   uncovered about 50 minutes, or until the
   chicken is no longer pink when cut.

Garlic-Glazed Leg of Lamb

Servings: 8

boneless leg of lamb, about 3½–4 pounds, rolled
and tied

Glaze:

    ⅓ cup dry sherry
    1 tablespoon paprika
    2 tablespoons soy sauce
    2 tablespoons olive oil
    4 cloves garlic, minced
    ⅓ cup water

1. Combine the glaze ingredients in a small bowl.
   Place the lamb on a rack in a shallow roasting
   pan, and brush with the glaze.
2. Roast for 2¾ to 3 hours at 325°F, brushing about
   every 20 minutes with the glaze.

Glazed Yule Ham

10–15 pound uncooked store-bought ham
orange marmalade
1 package (8-ounce) cream cheese, softened
greens of your choice (for garnish)

1. Follow package directions for baking ham.
   (Generally, baking takes $3\frac{1}{2}$ to 4 hours.)
2. Thirty minutes before ham is done, brush over
   with orange marmalade.
3. When ham is cooked, transfer it to a cutting
   board and cool slightly.
4. Using a pastry bag fitted with a
   star tip, pipe the cream cheese
   decoratively on top of ham.
   Slice and garnish with greens.

Herb Stuffing

4 ounces beef suet, finely chopped
1 cup seasoned bread crumbs
1 tablespoon dried parsley
1 tablespoon dried sage
dash of thyme
1 tablespoon grated lemon rind
pepper and salt to taste
1 large egg, lightly beaten
2 teaspoons milk

1. Mix suet with bread crumbs, parsley, sage, thyme, lemon rind, pepper, and salt.
2. Stir in beaten egg and milk. (Add more milk if necessary to attain your preferred consistency.)
3. Stuff poultry just prior to cooking. (You may wish to enlarge the quantities in the recipe if you are cooking a particularly large bird.)

Holiday Maple Ham

1¼ cups firmly packed dark brown sugar

⅓ cup maple syrup

whole cloves (quantity will depend on size of ham)

precooked ham (approximately 10 pounds),
   trimmed

1. Preheat oven to 350°F.
2. In a medium bowl, combine the brown sugar
   and the maple syrup and set aside.
3. Place ham on a rack in roasting pan.
   Set pan in center of the oven. Bake for 1 hour
   and 10 minutes.
4. Remove ham from oven. Using a kitchen knife,
   score the surface of the ham in a diamond pattern.
   Insert cloves evenly along top of the ham.
   Brush sugar and syrup mixture over the ham.
5. Return ham to oven; bake for 20 minutes more.

Holiday-Style Roast

Servings: 4

cooking oil

$1^{1}/_{2}$–$1^{3}/_{4}$ pound bottom round
   or boneless rump roast

1 can (16-ounce) crushed tomatoes

1 cup beef broth, fresh, canned,
   or prepared with beef bouillon

$^{1}/_{3}$ cup diced carrots

$^{1}/_{3}$ cup diced turnips

$^{1}/_{3}$ cup diced parsnips

3 small leeks, chopped
   (whites and light green)

2 tablespoons chopped fresh parsley

$^{1}/_{4}$ teaspoon thyme

4 black peppercorns

1 bay leaf

1. In a Dutch oven, heat a small amount of oil over medium heat. Add the beef and brown well on all sides.

2. Reduce the heat and add the tomatoes (undrained) and broth, then all remaining ingredients. Bring to a boil, then reduce heat to low.

3. At this point you can cover and simmer for about 3 hours on the stovetop, or cover and bake in a preheated 325°F oven for about 3 hours, or until fork-tender.

4. Remove the roast to a serving platter and keep warm. Increase the heat to medium-high and cook the vegetable mixture until it is reduced to no more than 2 cups. Remove the bay leaf and peppercorns.

5. Slice the roast, pour about half the sauce over the roast, and serve the remaining sauce on the side.

Mrs. Claus's Meatloaf

Servings: 6

1½ pounds lean ground beef or meatloaf mix

1 cup soft bread crumbs

½ cup chopped celery

⅓ cup chopped onion

½ teaspoon dry mustard

1 tablespoon dried parsley, optional

salt and pepper to taste

1 egg

¼ cup milk

1 tablespoon Worcestershire sauce

¼ cup ketchup

1. Preheat the oven to 350°F. Lightly grease an 8" · 11" baking dish.
2. Combine the meat, bread crumbs, celery, onion, mustard, parsley, salt, and pepper.
3. Beat the egg lightly and add the milk and Worcestershire sauce; add the liquid ingredients to the meat mixture. Combine well. Pat mixture into a loaf shape in the baking dish.
4. Bake for 45 minutes, then spread ketchup over the top of the loaf. Return to the oven to bake for an additional 15 minutes.

Roast Turkey with Apricot Fruit Stuffing

1½ cups chopped onions

5 tablespoons margarine

2 quarts cubed bread, toasted

¾ pound pitted prunes, sliced

6 dried apricot segments, coarsely chopped

2½ cups tart apples, peeled, cored, and chopped
  into 1-inch chunks

1 cup apple juice

2 teaspoons dried sage

1 teaspoon dried basil

2¼ teaspoons salt

¼ teaspoon pepper

1 turkey, ready to cook (approximately 13 pounds)

1. Preheat oven to 375°F.
2. Sauté onions in margarine until they are golden brown.
3. In a mixing bowl, toss bread with onions, prunes, apricots, apples, apple juice, and seasonings.
4. Spoon stuffing into turkey; fasten with poultry pins if necessary.
5. Roast for 25 minutes per pound. Scoop out fat from the pan as it gathers. Check regularly near the end of the allotted time; juices should run clear when bird is done. Do not overcook.

Sausage Poultry and Game Stuffing

³/₄ cup sausage, uncooked,
   casings removed, crumbled

2¹/₂ cups seasoned bread crumbs

4 cups water

1¹/₄ tablespoons dried parsley

1¹/₄ tablespoons dried onion

¹/₂ teaspoon pepper

2 large eggs, lightly beaten

¹/₃ cup butter, melted

1. In a skillet, brown sausage lightly. Remove sausage; drain on a paper towel.
2. Place bread crumbs in a large bowl and add water. When bread crumbs are soft, press out excess liquid by hand.
3. In a large bowl, combine sausage with soft bread crumbs, parsley, onion, pepper, and beaten eggs. Drizzle melted butter into the mixture.
4. Stuff poultry just prior to cooking. (You may wish to enlarge the quantities in the recipe if you are cooking a particularly large bird.)

Scalloped Apples and Pork Chops

Servings: 4

2$\frac{1}{2}$ cups sliced apples

4 small sweet potatoes, pared and sliced

$\frac{1}{3}$ cup raisins

$\frac{1}{3}$ cup brown sugar

dash nutmeg

3 tablespoons currant jelly

3 tablespoons prepared mustard

4 pork chops, cut $\frac{3}{4}$-inch thick

salt and pepper

1. Preheat oven to 350°F. Grease an 8" · 11" baking dish.
2. Place half the apples at either end of the baking dish. In the center, place the sweet potato slices. Scatter the raisins over all, and sprinkle with brown sugar and nutmeg.
3. Combine the jelly and mustard, mixing until smooth.
4. Trim fat from chops and coat both sides of each with the jelly mixture. Place chops on the sweet potatoes and sprinkle with salt and pepper.
5. Cover and bake 1 hour and 40 minutes, or until the chops are tender.

Special Cornbread Sausage Stuffing

Yield: stuffs a 10-pound turkey

1 pound pork or turkey sausage

1 cup chopped onion

$^1/_2$ cup chopped celery

$^1/_2$ cup chopped green pepper

3 cups coarsely crumbled cornbread

3 cups dried bread cubes

1 teaspoon poultry seasoning,

   or $^1/_2$ teaspoon sage and $^1/_2$ teaspoon thyme

$^1/_4$ teaspoon pepper

$^1/_3$ cup butter

chicken broth or water (up to 1 cup)

1. In a large skillet, brown sausage, onion, celery, and green pepper. Drain well.
2. Combine sausage mixture with the cornbread and bread cubes, and sprinkle with seasonings.
3. Melt the butter and drizzle it over the stuffing. Add broth until the mixture is evenly moist, but not wet.
4. To bake separately, place in a lightly greased 3-quart baking dish and bake, covered, at 325°F for about 45 minutes.

Stuffed Pork Tenderloin

Servings: 4

1¼ pound pork tenderloin

2 tablespoons butter

1 cup packaged dry-herb–flavored or
sage-and-onion–flavored stuffing mix, or 1 cup
small dry bread cubes plus ¼ teaspoon
poultry seasoning

½ cup chopped apple

2 tablespoons raisins

2 tablespoons apple juice

salt and pepper to taste

1. Preheat oven to 350°F.
2. Slice the tenderloin lengthwise, but do not cut completely through. Spread the halves open. Place plastic wrap over them, and use a meat mallet to flatten to an even thickness.
3. Melt the butter and combine with the bread stuffing, apple, raisins, and apple juice. Add salt and pepper to taste.
4. Spread the stuffing over the pork to within $^{1}/_{2}$ inch of all edges. Beginning from the short end, roll the tenderloin like a jelly roll. Tie securely in three places with white kitchen string.
5. Bake for 45–50 minutes, or until a meat thermometer reads 160°F.
6. After removing from the oven, allow to stand (covered with foil) for about 15 minutes before slicing.

Sweet and Sour Chicken

3 pounds boneless chicken breast,
   cut into 1-inch pieces
1 green pepper, sliced into strips
2 tablespoons vegetable oil
$\frac{1}{4}$ teaspoon salt
$\frac{1}{4}$ teaspoon pepper
$\frac{1}{4}$ teaspoon garlic powder
$\frac{1}{4}$ teaspoon parsley flakes
1 can (8-ounce) chunk pineapple, drained
1 jar (4-ounce) maraschino cherries
1 jar (12-ounce) prepared sweet and sour sauce

1. In a skillet, sauté chicken and sliced pepper in the oil
   until chicken turns golden. Drain off grease.
2. Sprinkle with salt, pepper, garlic powder, and parsley.
3. Add fruit and sweet and sour sauce to chicken.
4. Cook chicken mixture over medium heat until mixture
   is heated throughout.

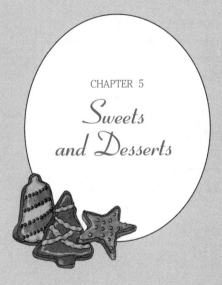

CHAPTER 5

*Sweets
and Desserts*

Anise Oval Cookies

²/₃ cup granulated sugar

²/₃ cup solid vegetable shortening

2 large eggs

2 teaspoons anise flavor extract

2 cups all-purpose flour

2 teaspoons baking powder

1 cup sifted confectioners' sugar

1–2 tablespoons hot water or milk

¹/₂ teaspoon vanilla extract

green and red food coloring

1. Preheat oven to 350°F.
2. In a large mixing bowl, cream together sugar and shortening, at medium mixer speed, until light and fluffy.
3. Blend in eggs and anise extract.
4. At low speed, beat in flour and baking powder.
5. Shape dough into 2-inch ovals. Place ovals at least 1 inch apart on ungreased cookie sheets.
6. Bake cookies until golden brown, approximately 8–10 minutes. Transfer baking sheet to a wire rack to cool.
7. For icing: In a large bowl, mix confectioners' sugar, hot water or milk, vanilla extract, and food coloring. Drizzle over the cookies while they are cooling.
8. Store cookies wrapped in wax paper in an airtight container.

Apple Accompaniment

Yield: about 2 cups

3 tablespoons butter

2 cups sliced or coarsely chopped apple

2 tablespoons packed brown sugar

$1/2$ teaspoon cinnamon

$1/4$ cup water

1. In a medium skillet, melt the butter over medium-high heat (do not allow to brown), and sauté the apples for 2–3 minutes.

2. In a small bowl, mix the brown sugar, cinnamon, and water.

3. Add the mixture to the apples, reduce heat to low, and continue cooking an additional 2–3 minutes. Apples should be tender but remain firm.

4. Use as a topping for pancakes or an accompaniment to eggs or ham. Also a great ice cream topping!

5. Seasoning variation: Add $\frac{1}{4}$ teaspoon pumpkin pie spice to the cinnamon.

Apple Crisp

Topping:

    3 tablespoons chilled butter

    $\frac{1}{2}$ cup firmly packed brown sugar

    $\frac{1}{3}$ cup all-purpose flour

In a medium bowl, mix together brown sugar, flour, and butter using a pastry blender or 2 knives, until coarse crumbs form.

Filling:

    $\frac{1}{2}$ teaspoon nutmeg

    $\frac{1}{2}$ teaspoon ground cinnamon

    $\frac{1}{4}$ cup water

    2 tablespoons granulated sugar

    4 cups apples, peeled, cored, and thinly sliced

1. Preheat oven to 375°F. Grease a 9" pie pan.
2. Place apples in prepared pan.
3. Mix together sugar, nutmeg, cinnamon, and water.
4. Toss apples with sugar mixture.
5. Sprinkle topping over filling.
6. Cook until top is golden brown and crispy, approximately 30 minutes.

Banana Split Cake

3 sticks butter or margarine, softened
2 cups crushed graham crackers
2 large eggs
2 cups confectioners' sugar
5 bananas, sliced very thin
8 ounces nondairy whipped topping
1 jar (4-ounce) maraschino cherries, drained
$^1/_2$ cup coarsely chopped pecans
1 can (20-ounce) crushed pineapple, drained

1. Mix 1 stick butter with graham cracker crumbs. Pat mixture into the bottom of a 9" × 13" pan.
2. Beat eggs, remaining butter, confectioners' sugar, and banana pieces for no less than 15 minutes.
3. Spread batter over prepared crust.
4. Cover with whipped topping, sprinkle with nuts and cherries. Spread crushed pineapple over whipped topping.
5. Chill overnight.

Brandy Rings

2¹/₂ cups sifted all-purpose flour
1 cup butter or margarine
2 tablespoons brandy

1. Preheat oven to 350°F. Grease 2 large baking sheets.
2. Combine the flour, margarine and brandy in a large mixing bowl, and blend together to make dough.
3. On a lightly floured surface, roll the dough into ropes approximately ¹/₂ inch thick.
4. Cut the ropes into 5-inch strips. Twist two pieces together; shape into a ring; pinch ends together to seal.
5. Repeat with the remaining dough.
6. Place the rings a good distance apart on prepared baking sheets. Bake rings until golden, approximately 12–15 minutes.

Caramel Chocolates

2¹/₂ tablespoons butter

2 cups molasses

1 cup firmly packed dark brown sugar

1 teaspoon vanilla extract

¹/₂ cup milk

3 ounces semisweet chocolate, coarsely chopped

1. In medium saucepan, melt butter over medium heat.
2. Add molasses, brown sugar, vanilla, and milk. Stir until sugar is dissolved.
3. Bring mixture to a simmer; add chocolate, stirring until melted and smooth.
4. Bring chocolate mixture to a boil. Remove from heat for a moment and test: When a small amount of mixture is dropped into cold water and a firm ball is formed, proceed to next step. Do not overcook!
5. Pour mixture into medium-size buttered pan. Let stand and cool; cut into small squares.

Chocolate Crinkles

1/2 cup vegetable oil

4 ounces unsweetened chocolate, melted

2 cups granulated sugar

4 large eggs

2 teaspoons vanilla

2 cups all-purpose flour

2 teaspoons baking powder

1/2 teaspoon salt

1 cup confectioners' sugar

1. In a large mixing bowl, mix oil, melted chocolate, and granulated sugar.
2. Beat in eggs, 1 at a time, beating well after each addition.
3. Add vanilla. Beat in flour, baking powder, and salt.
4. Cover bowl with plastic wrap. Chill for several hours.
5. When ready to bake, preheat oven to 350°F. Grease 2 medium baking sheets.
6. Drop dough by teaspoonfuls into confectioners' sugar. Roll dough in sugar and shape into balls.
7. Bake for 10–12 minutes until set.

Christmas Chocolate Pudding Cake

Yield: 9-inch cake

1 cup flour
1¼ cups granulated sugar, divided
2 teaspoons baking powder
⅛ teaspoon salt
½ cup cocoa powder, divided
¼ cup butter
½ cup milk
1 teaspoon vanilla
½ cup brown sugar
1½ cups cold water

1. Preheat oven to 350°F. Grease a 9" baking pan.
2. Stir together the flour, $^3/_4$ cup of the granulated sugar, baking powder, salt, and $^1/_4$ cup of the cocoa.
3. Melt the butter and combine with the milk and vanilla; then add to the dry ingredients, mixing just until blended. Turn batter into baking pan.
4. Over the top of the batter, sprinkle the brown sugar, then the remaining $^1/_2$ cup granulated sugar, then the remaining $^1/_4$ cup cocoa. Pour the water over all.
5. Bake 40 minutes. Allow to cool at room temperature before serving.

Variation: For mocha pudding cake, substitute strong cold coffee for the cold water.

Christmas Cowboy Coffeecake

Yield: 8-inch cake

1¼ cups flour

¼ teaspoon salt

1 cup brown sugar

⅓ cup shortening

1 teaspoon baking powder

¼ teaspoon baking soda

¼ teaspoon cinnamon

⅛ teaspoon nutmeg

1 egg

½ cup soured milk or buttermilk

1. Preheat the oven to 375°F. Grease and flour an 8" square or round cake pan.
2. Combine flour, salt, and sugar; cut in the shortening until the mixture has a crumb-like texture.
3. Remove and reserve 1/4 cup of the mixture.
4. To the remaining mixture, stir in the baking powder, baking soda, and spices.
5. Beat the egg well; mix it with the milk. Add to the dry ingredients, and mix quickly but thoroughly.
6. Pour into the baking pan and top with reserved crumb mixture. Bake 25–30 minutes.

Christmas Theme Sugar Cookies

1 cup granulated sugar
1 cup margarine
1 large egg
$\frac{1}{2}$ teaspoon almond or vanilla extract
$1\frac{1}{2}$ teaspoons baking powder
$\frac{1}{2}$ teaspoon salt
$2\frac{1}{2}$ cups all-purpose flour
red and green sugar crystals
colored jimmies
small silver ball candies

1. In a large mixing bowl, beat together the margarine and sugar.
2. Beat in the egg, extract, baking powder, and salt. Gradually add in the flour; mix well.

3. On a floured surface, knead dough by hand and shape into a large ball. Wrap in plastic wrap and chill up to two hours, until firm.

4. When ready to bake, preheat oven to 350°F. Grease a cookie or baking sheet.

5. Roll out dough on a floured surface to ¼-inch thickness. Cut out shapes with Christmas theme cookie cutters. Gather trimmings; roll out again, and cut more cookies.

6. Decorate with sugar crystals, jimmies, and candies.

7. Bake each batch for approximately 10–12 minutes, or until lightly browned.

Note: Bake large cookies with other large ones and small cookies with other small ones for best results. Placing cookies of unlike sizes on the same sheet will result in uneven cooking.

Classic Christmas Carrot Cake

Yield: large bundt cake

3 cups flour

2 cups sugar

2 teaspoons baking soda

1 teaspoon cinnamon

$\frac{1}{2}$ teaspoon salt

3 eggs

2 teaspoons vanilla

$1\frac{1}{2}$ cups vegetable oil

1 can (8-ounce) crushed pineapple (undrained)

2 cups grated carrots

$1\frac{1}{2}$ cups chopped walnuts

$\frac{1}{2}$ cup coconut

cream cheese frosting

1. Preheat oven to 350°F. Grease and flour a bundt cake pan.
2. In a large bowl, stir together the dry ingredients.
3. Beat the eggs lightly, and add with the vanilla and oil to the dry ingredients, beating well.
4. Stir in the undrained pineapple and the carrots, then the nuts and coconut.
5. Turn into the bundt cake pan and bake for 1 hour, or until a toothpick or knife inserted in the middle comes out clean.
6. Cool, then frost with cream cheese frosting. If desired, sprinkle frosting with chopped walnuts or coconut, or both.

Coconut Wreath Cookies

$^{1}/_{2}$ cup butter or margarine, softened

$^{1}/_{2}$ cup granulated sugar

1 large egg

1 package (3$^{1}/_{2}$-ounce) of shredded sweetened
coconut

1$^{3}/_{4}$ cups all-purpose flour

red and green candied cherries, sliced

1. In a large bowl, beat together butter and sugar.
2. Blend in the egg and coconut. On low speed, add flour, $\frac{1}{2}$ cup at a time, until completely blended.
3. Wrap dough in plastic wrap and chill for several hours.
4. When ready to bake, preheat oven to 375°F. Lightly grease and flour a baking sheet.
5. On a floured surface, roll $\frac{1}{3}$ of the dough at a time to a $\frac{1}{4}$-inch thickness. Using a $2\frac{1}{2}$-inch doughnut cutter, cut dough into rings. Gather trimmings; roll the dough, and cut out more cookies.
6. Remove any excess coconut from the edges; edges of cookies should be smooth.
7. Place cookies on prepared baking sheet 1 inch apart. Arrange cherry slices on the cookies to resemble flower petals; press into the cookies.
8. Bake in batches for approximately 10 minutes, or until lightly browned.

Crunchy Christmas Candy

1 cup granulated sugar
$\frac{1}{2}$ cup evaporated milk
$\frac{1}{4}$ cup margarine
$\frac{1}{4}$ cup crunchy peanut butter
$\frac{1}{2}$ teaspoon vanilla extract
1 cup old-fashioned dry oats
$\frac{1}{2}$ cup peanuts

1. In a large saucepan, bring sugar, evaporated milk, and margarine to a boil, stirring frequently.
2. When sugar is dissolved, remove from heat, and stir in peanut butter and vanilla.
3. Mix in oats and peanuts. Drop mixture by rounded teaspoonfuls onto wax paper so that each morsel has a peak. (If mixture is too stiff, add a few drops of milk.)
4. Chill candy until firm.

Crunchy Christmas Nut Treats

1 cup solid vegetable shortening
¼ cup confectioners' sugar
1 teaspoon vanilla extract
2 cups sifted all-purpose flour
½ cup chopped almonds
½ cup chopped walnuts

1. Preheat oven to 300°F.
2. In a large bowl, beat together shortening, sugar, and vanilla extract. At low speed, beat in the flour. Stir in the nuts.
3. Shape dough into round balls, and place them several inches apart on an ungreased cookie sheet.
4. Bake in batches for 15–18 minutes. Check frequently near end of cooking time; do not scorch.
5. Transfer cookies to a wire rack. Roll warm cookies in additional confectioners' sugar.
6. Let stand until cool, about 30 minutes.

Decadent Chocolate Amaretto Cheesecake

Yield: 10-inch cheescake

Crust:

- 1/4 cup butter
- 1 cup graham cracker crumbs
- 1/4 cup cocoa powder
- 2 tablespoons sugar

Filling:

- 8 ounces semisweet chocolate
- 16 ounces cream cheese
- 1/2 cup sugar
- 3 large eggs
- 8 ounces sour cream
- 1 teaspoon vanilla
- 1 teaspoon almond extract
- 1/3 cup amaretto liqueur

1. Preheat the oven to 300°F.

2. To make the crust: Melt the butter and combine with other crust ingredients. Press the mixture into the bottom and 1 inch up the sides of a 10" springform pan.

3. To make the filling: Melt the chocolate and set it aside to cool.

4. Soften the cream cheese and beat it with the sugar until the mixture is smooth.

5. Add the eggs, one at a time, beating well after each addition. Stir in the sour cream, melted chocolate, vanilla, almond extract, and amaretto.

6. Turn the mixture into the crust and bake for 1 hour. Turn the oven off and let the cheesecake cool in the oven for 1 hour.

7. Remove to a rack and allow to cool completely; then cover loosely and chill for at least 12 hours.

Gingerbread from Home

$\frac{1}{2}$ cup firmly packed light brown sugar

$\frac{1}{3}$ cup butter

1 teaspoon baking soda

$\frac{1}{2}$ cup light molasses

$1\frac{1}{4}$ cup all-purpose flour

1 teaspoon ground cinnamon

$\frac{1}{2}$ teaspoon ground ginger

1 large egg

$\frac{1}{2}$ cup boiling water

1. Preheat oven to 325°F. Grease and flour an 8" square baking pan.
2. In a large bowl, combine brown sugar and butter. Add baking soda and molasses.
3. Add flour, cinnamon, and ginger and mix well.
4. Add in egg and mix well.
5. Add boiling water. Mix until thoroughly blended.
6. Pour batter into prepared pan and smooth the top. Bake gingerbread until a toothpick inserted into the center comes out clean, approximately 40 minutes.

Gingerbread Men

¹/₂ cup granulated sugar

¹/₂ cup solid vegetable shortening

1 large egg

¹/₂ teaspoon salt

1 teaspoon baking powder

¹/₂ teaspoon baking soda

1 teaspoon ground ginger

1¹/₂ teaspoons ground
cinnamon

1 teaspoon ground cloves

¹/₂ cup light molasses

2¹/₄ cups all-purpose flour

prepared frosting, green and red

1. In a large mixing bowl, beat together sugar and shortening.

2. Add egg, salt, baking powder, baking soda, ginger, cinnamon, cloves, and molasses.

3. Add flour, ½ cup at a time, beating until dough forms.

4. Shape dough into a ball, wrap in plastic wrap, and chill for up to two hours, or until firm.

5. When ready to bake, preheat oven to 350°F.

6. On a floured surface, roll out dough to ¼-inch thickness. Using gingerbread man cookie cutter, cut out cookies. Place them on an ungreased cookie sheet at least 1 inch apart.

7. Bake cookies in batches for 8–10 minutes for small men, 12–15 minutes for larger ones. Transfer baking sheet to a wire rack to cool.

8. Spread frosting over cookies. Decorate with candies.

Green and Red Chewy Chocolate Cookies

1¼ cups margarine, softened

2 cups granulated sugar

2 large eggs

2 teaspoons vanilla extract

2 cups all-purpose flour

¾ cup cocoa powder (not instant)

1 teaspoon baking soda

1 teaspoon salt

green and red candy-coated chocolates to taste
(we like a lot of them)

1. Preheat oven to 350°F.
2. Beat together margarine and sugar until light and fluffy.
3. Add eggs and vanilla. Beat in flour, cocoa, baking soda, and salt.
4. Stir in candy-coated chocolates.
5. Drop batter by rounded teaspoonfuls onto ungreased baking sheet.
6. Cook in batches for 8–10 minutes per sheet of cookies. Check cookies near end of baking time. Do not overcook!
7. Transfer baking sheet to wire rack to cool.

Hermits

2 cups sifted all-purpose flour

2 teaspoons baking powder

1 teaspoon ground cinnamon

$\frac{1}{4}$ teaspoon nutmeg

1 teaspoon mace

$\frac{1}{2}$ cup butter or margarine

$\frac{1}{2}$ cup firmly packed dark brown sugar

$\frac{1}{2}$ cup granulated sugar

2 large eggs, lightly beaten

2 cups dark raisins

$\frac{1}{2}$ cup almonds

1. Preheat oven to 350°F. Grease a 9" × 13" baking dish.
2. Sift flour, baking powder, cinnamon, nutmeg, and mace together. (We suggest 3 times.)
3. In a large bowl, beat together butter and sugar until light and fluffy.
4. Beat dry ingredients into butter mixture.
5. Beat in eggs.
6. Stir in raisins and nuts.
7. Pour the mixture into prepared dish. Bake hermits until browned, approximately 15 minutes.
8. Transfer baking pan to a wire rack to cool.

Holiday Baked Custard

1 cup milk
1 cup evaporated milk
3 large eggs, lightly beaten
¼ cup granulated sugar
¼ teaspoon salt
¼ teaspoon vanilla extract
water

1. Preheat oven to 325°F.
2. Combine all ingredients. Mix well.
3. Pour into medium-sized baking dish.
4. Place filled baking dish in a larger pan partially filled with cold water (about 1 inch deep).
5. Bake custard until set, approximately 50–60 minutes, checking frequently near end of allotted time. Do not overcook!

Holiday Baked Rice Pudding

Servings: 4–5

4 cups 2% milk
4 large eggs
2 cups cooked rice
$\frac{1}{2}$ cup sugar
$\frac{1}{4}$ teaspoon salt
$\frac{1}{2}$ cup raisins
1 teaspoon vanilla
dash of nutmeg

1. Preheat oven to 350°F.
2. Heat the milk until it's very warm, but not boiling; place it in a 3-quart baking dish.
3. With an electric mixer, beat the eggs until light yellow and fluffy.
4. Add the rice, sugar, salt, raisins, and vanilla. Pour mixture into the baking dish and stir slightly. Sprinkle with nutmeg.
5. Place the dish in another shallow baking dish with $1\frac{1}{2}$ inches of water. Bake for 45–60 minutes, or until pudding is set.

Holiday Fudge

4¹/₂ cups granulated sugar
1 can evaporated milk
¹/₄ cup butter
12 ounces of milk chocolate bar
12 ounces chocolate chips
1 tablespoon vanilla extract
¹/₈ teaspoon salt
1 pint marshmallow spread
2 cups walnuts, coarsely chopped

1. Grease a 13" × 9" pan.
2. In a large saucepan, cook sugar, milk, and butter for 5 minutes, stirring constantly.
3. Dissolve chocolate bar and chocolate chips in saucepan.
4. Mix in vanilla, salt, marshmallow, and walnuts.
5. Pour fudge into prepared pan.
6. Chill overnight.

Holiday Pound Cake

Yield: large tube cake

1 cup butter
5 eggs
2 cups sugar
2 cups flour
1 teaspoon vanilla, almond, or citrus extract

1. Preheat oven to 300°F. Generously butter a large tube pan.
2. Cream the butter well. Add the eggs, one at a time, beating 1 minute after each addition.
3. While beating continuously, gradually add the sugar, then the flour, then the flavoring.
4. Pour into the tube pan and bake for $1^1/_2$–$1^3/_4$ hours, or until a toothpick or knife inserted in the middle comes out clean.
5. Serve with strawberries or other berries, if desired.

Lemon Bars

1 cup all-purpose flour

$^1/_4$ cup confectioners' sugar

$^1/_2$ cup butter, softened

2 large eggs, lightly beaten

$^3/_4$ cup granulated sugar

3 tablespoons fresh lemon juice

2 tablespoons all-purpose flour

$^1/_2$ teaspoon baking powder

confectioners' sugar

1. Preheat oven to 350°F. Grease an 8" × 8" × 2" pan.
2. Mix together flour and confectioners' sugar. Using a pastry blender, cut butter into flour mixture until coarse crumbs form.
3. Pat crumb mixture into prepared pan.
4. Bake crust until golden, approximately 10–12 minutes. Set aside.
5. In a large bowl, combine beaten eggs with sugar and lemon juice. Beat until thickened.
6. Beat in flour and baking powder.
7. Pour batter over prepared crust.
8. Return pan to oven; bake lemon bars until set, approximately 20–25 minutes.
9. Cool slightly. Sift confectioners' sugar over top. When completely cool, cut into 1-inch squares.

Maple Bells

1 cup butter or margarine, softened
¾ cup firmly packed light brown sugar
2 large eggs
½ cup maple syrup
2 teaspoons cream of tartar
1 teaspoon baking soda
¼ teaspoon salt
4 cups all-purpose flour

1. In a large mixing bowl, beat together butter and sugar at medium speed until light and fluffy.

2. Beat in eggs and maple syrup. Beat in cream of tartar, baking soda, and salt.

3. At low speed, beat in flour until dough forms.

4. Shape dough into a ball; wrap in plastic wrap and refrigerate for 1 hour.

5. When ready to bake, preheat oven to 350°F. Grease a baking sheet.

6. On a floured surface, roll out dough to a $\frac{1}{8}$" thickness; using bell-shaped cookie cutters, cut out cookies. Place cookies in batches on prepared baking sheet.

7. All large pieces should be baked together, as should all small ones, so that each batch will cook evenly.

8. Bake cookies until golden brown, approximately 10 minutes.

Meatless Mince Pie

prepared uncooked double layer pie crust

$\frac{1}{2}$ cup cooked rice

$\frac{1}{2}$ cup seedless raisins

$\frac{1}{2}$ cup currants

$\frac{1}{2}$ cup honey

2 tablespoons chopped orange sections

1 tablespoon grated lemon peel

1 tablespoon butter

$\frac{1}{8}$ teaspoon cinnamon

$\frac{1}{8}$ teaspoon nutmeg

1 large egg white, lightly beaten

sprinkling of granulated sugar

1. Preheat oven to 450°F. Grease a medium-sized pie pan.

2. Mix together rice, raisins, currants, honey, orange, lemon peel, butter, cinnamon, and nutmeg.

3. Place pie crust into the pie pan. Fill with the rice mixture. Cover with remaining pie crust and press edges together to seal. Brush pie with beaten egg white. Sprinkle with sugar.

4. Bake pie until crust is golden, approximately 10 minutes. Reduce temperature to 350°F; bake about 30 minutes more. Check frequently; do not scorch or overcook!

5. Transfer pan to a wire rack to cool.

Old-Fashioned Christmas Tea Cakes

1 cup granulated sugar
1 cup margarine
3 large eggs
1 teaspoon nutmeg
3½ cups all-purpose flour

1. Preheat oven to 350°F. Grease a baking sheet.
2. In a large bowl, beat together sugar and margarine until light and fluffy.
3. Beat in eggs and nutmeg. Beat in flour ½ cup at a time, beating until blended and smooth.
4. Drop batter by rounded tablespoonfuls onto a floured surface. Roll cakes out to ¼" thickness.
5. Place cakes 1 inch apart on prepared baking sheet.
6. Bake cakes in batches until golden and set, approximately 10 minutes.
7. Transfer baking sheet to a wire rack to cool.

Peanut Popcorn Fudge

$\frac{1}{2}$ cup smooth peanut butter

$\frac{1}{2}$ cup milk

2 cups granulated sugar

1 tablespoon margarine

heaping cup of popped popcorn, coarsely chopped

1 teaspoon vanilla extract

1. Grease a medium-sized baking dish.
2. In medium saucepan, warm peanut butter, milk, and sugar until smooth.
3. Add margarine, popcorn, and vanilla.
4. Beat until all ingredients are well distributed and mixture is of an even consistency.
5. Pour into prepared baking dish; chill well.

Peppermint Flavored Candy Cane Cookies

1¼ cups margarine
1 cup confectioners' sugar
1 teaspoon vanilla extract
¼ teaspoon salt
1 large egg
3½ cups all-purpose flour
¼ teaspoon peppermint extract
several drops of red food coloring

1. Preheat oven to 350°F. Grease a baking sheet.
2. Beat together margarine and sugar on medium speed until light and fluffy.
3. Mix in vanilla, salt, and egg. On low speed, beat in flour ½ cup at a time, until dough begins to form.

4. Shape dough into a ball and divide in half.

5. In a small bowl, mix red food coloring and peppermint extract. Knead food coloring mixture into one half of the dough.

6. With lightly floured hands, roll 1 teaspoon of plain dough into a 4-inch rope.

7. Repeat rolling process with red dough. Braid ropes together and shape as a candy cane. Pinch ends together to seal.

8. Repeat with remaining dough.

9. Place cookies at least 1 inch apart on prepared baking sheet. Bake in batches for 10 minutes, or until golden brown.

10. Transfer baking sheet to a wire rack to cool. Let stand until cool, about 20 minutes.

"Perfect Every Time" Toll House Cookies

6 cups all-purpose flour

2 teaspoons baking soda

1 teaspoon salt

1¼ cup solid vegetable shortening

2 cups firmly packed dark brown sugar

1 cup granulated sugar

¾ cup butter

4 teaspoons vanilla extract

4 large eggs, lightly beaten

1 large bag chocolate chips

2 cups coarsely chopped pecans

1. Preheat oven to 375°F. Grease a large baking sheet.
2. Mix together flour, baking soda, and salt and keep to the side.
3. In a large mixing bowl, beat together shortening, sugar, and butter at medium speed until light and fluffy.
4. Beat in vanilla and eggs.
5. Using low speed, beat in flour mixture $\frac{1}{2}$ cup at a time, beating until dough forms.
6. Stir in the chocolate chips and nuts.
7. Bake cookies in batches until golden brown, approximately 10–12 minutes.
8. Let stand until cool.

Plum Pudding Pie

prepared unbaked pie shell to fit your standard
  pie pan

2 large eggs

1 cup orange marmalade

1 cup pitted dates, coarsely chopped

1 cup shredded sweetened coconut

1 cup crystallized fruit, chopped
  (preferably crystallized plums)

1 cup walnuts, coarsely chopped

$^1/_4$ cup slivers of ginger-preserved
  watermelon rind (if available)

2 tablespoons milk

1 tablespoon butter

1. Preheat oven to 425°F.
2. Beat together eggs; add marmalade, dates, coconut, crystallized fruit, walnuts, watermelon rind, and milk, in that order. Blend well.
3. Place pie crust in greased pie pan. (Or, if crust comes in aluminum pie pan, use that.) Pour filling into prepared crust.
4. Dot top with butter.
5. Bake for 25 minutes, or until crust is golden-brown.

Hint: If pie seems dry during baking, gently mix in
   1 tablespoon of orange or pineapple juice.

Potato Cookies

1 stick butter or margarine
1 cup granulated sugar
1 large egg, lightly beaten
1 cup instant potato buds
1½ cup prepared biscuit mix
½ cup shredded sweetened coconut
1 tablespoon coconut or vanilla extract
confectioners' sugar

1. Preheat oven to 350°F. Grease a large baking sheet.
2. In a large bowl, beat together butter and sugar until light and fluffy.
3. Add egg to butter mixture.
4. Mix in potato buds, biscuit mix, shredded coconut, and coconut or vanilla extract.
5. Drop by rounded teaspoonfuls onto prepared cookie sheet. Flatten cookies with the back of a fork.
6. Bake cookies for 5 minutes. Remove baking sheet from oven. Sprinkle with confectioners' sugar.
7. Return to oven for 5 minutes more.
8. Let stand until cool.

Prancer's Pecan Pie

prepared uncooked pie crust to fit standard pie pan

3 large eggs

$^1/_2$ cup granulated sugar

1 cup coarsely chopped pecan
   pieces, toasted

1 teaspoon vanilla extract

1 cup dark corn syrup

$^1/_2$ teaspoon salt

1. Preheat oven to 350°F.
2. Place pie crust in greased pie pan (or, if crust comes in aluminum pie pan, use that); put in oven and brown slightly, 5–10 minutes. Remove from the oven.
3. In a large bowl, beat eggs until foamy. Add sugar, pecans, vanilla, corn syrup, and salt. Mix well.
4. Pour filling into prepared crust.
5. Bake pie until top is set, approximately 40–45 minutes.
6. Transfer pan to a wire rack to cool.

Santa's Special Waldorf Salad

Servings: 6

$\frac{1}{2}$ cup mayonnaise

1 tablespoon sugar

1 teaspoon lemon juice

salt to taste

2 cups diced red-skinned apples

1 cup finely sliced celery

$\frac{1}{2}$ cup coarsely chopped walnuts

1. Blend the mayonnaise with the sugar, lemon juice, and salt.
2. Combine the apples, celery, and nuts, and fold in the dressing mixture.
3. Chill before serving.

Special Christmas Oatmeal Cookies

1 stick butter or margarine

4 tablespoons solid vegetable shortening

1 cup firmly packed light brown sugar

$\frac{1}{2}$ cup granulated sugar

1 large egg

$\frac{1}{4}$ cup water

1 teaspoon vanilla extract

3 cups old-fashioned rolled oats

1 cup all-purpose flour

1 teaspoon salt

$\frac{1}{2}$ teaspoon baking soda

1 teaspoon ground cinnamon

$\frac{1}{2}$ cup chocolate morsels

macadamia nuts, walnuts, and raisins in
   desired amounts

1. Preheat oven to 350°F. Grease a large baking sheet.
2. Beat butter and shortening together until mixture is smooth.
3. Beat in sugar, egg, water, and vanilla until light and fluffy.
4. Add remaining ingredients. Mix well.
5. Drop mixture by rounded teaspoonfuls onto prepared baking sheet.
6. Bake cookies in batches until golden-brown, approximately 12–15 minutes.
7. Transfer cookies to a wire rack to cool.

St. Nicholas Day Candies

1 cup pitted, chopped dates

1 cup dark seedless raisins

$\frac{1}{2}$ cup figs, coarsely chopped

$\frac{1}{2}$ cup pitted dried apricots, coarsely chopped

$\frac{1}{2}$ cup orange peel

1 cup coarsely chopped walnuts

3 tablespoons fresh orange juice

shredded sweetened coconut

red or green plastic wrap

1. In a blender or food processor, process dried fruit and orange peel until ground to a uniform consistency.

2. Spoon the fruit mixture into a large bowl; stir in the walnuts and enough orange juice to hold the mix together. (Discard any excess orange juice.)

3. When mixture is sturdy enough, roll candy mixture into small balls, approximately 1 inch in diameter.

4. Roll balls in coconut. Wrap each candy individually in green or red plastic wrap and chill completely.

Trifle

1½ dozen ladyfingers, split in half

¼ cup sherry

1 dozen almond macaroon cookies, broken into pieces

¼ cup toasted almond slices

¾ cup fresh strawberries, sliced

¾ cup fresh peaches, sliced

¾ cup fresh blueberries, sliced

1 cup prepared custard (see recipe)

1 pint whipped cream

1. In a trifle bowl, arrange ladyfingers.
2. Sprinkle sherry over ladyfingers.
3. Add one layer of macaroon cookie pieces and half of the toasted almond slices.
4. Add one layer of strawberries, peaches, and blueberries.
5. Top with custard and whipped cream. Garnish with more almond slices.

Custard:

> 3 cups milk
>
> 3 large eggs
>
> 1¼ cups granulated sugar
>
> ⅓ cup all-purpose flour
>
> ¼ teaspoon salt
>
> 1 teaspoon vanilla extract
>
> ½ stick butter

1. Scald milk in top of large double boiler.
2. In a mixing bowl, beat eggs, sugar, flour, and salt at medium speed until light and fluffy.
3. Add egg mixture to scalded milk; cook over medium heat and stir constantly until thickened.
4. Add vanilla and butter. Stir till well blended.
5. Place a piece of wax paper directly over top of the surface. Cool for 30 minutes.

Waldorf-Style Holiday Fruit Salad

Servings: 6

2 unpeeled Red Delicious apples,
  cored and cubed
24 red grapes
24 green grapes
2 oranges, sectioned
1 cup plain yogurt
1 tablespoon honey
lettuce leaves
2 bananas, sliced
1/4 cup chopped walnuts

1. In a bowl, toss together the apples, grapes, and orange
2. In a small bowl, stir together the yogurt and honey.
   Mix into the fruit, tossing to coat evenly.
3. To serve, place lettuce leaves on each plate, and plac
   the fruit mixture on the lettuce.
4. Place the bananas around the edge of the plates, and
   sprinkle the walnuts over all.

Winter Sweet Potato Pudding

2 cups cooked sweet potatoes
1/4 cup unsweetened frozen apple juice
1/3 cup fresh orange juice
1 sliced banana
2 large eggs
1 teaspoon ground cinnamon

1. Preheat oven to 350°F. Grease a medium-sized pie pan.
2. Place all ingredients in a blender and process until smooth.
3. Pour mixture into prepared pie pan.
4. Bake pudding until top is set, approximately 35 minutes.
5. Transfer pan to wire rack; let cool.

Wish Cookies

10 graham crackers, crushed
$^{1}/_{2}$ cup butter or margarine, melted
$^{1}/_{2}$ cup chopped almonds
6 ounces chocolate chips
$^{1}/_{2}$ cup sweetened shredded coconut
1 can (12-ounce) sweetened condensed milk

1. Preheat oven to 350°F.
2. In a large mixing bowl, combine melted butter with graham crackers. Mix well.
3. Press crumb mixture into the bottom of a 13" × 9" pan.
4. Sprinkle nuts, then chocolate chips, and coconut (in that order) over cracker crumbs.
5. Gently pour condensed milk over the top.
6. Bake for 15–20 minutes, or until golden brown. Let cool before cutting.

CHAPTER 6

Drinks

Brandy Cocoa

2 tablespoons unsweetened cocoa powder

$\frac{1}{3}$ cup granulated sugar

$1\frac{1}{2}$ cups boiling water

4 cups whole milk

3 teaspoons brandy

1. In a saucepan, scald the milk.
2. In another saucepan, mix the cocoa, sugar, and enough boiling water to make a smooth paste.
3. Add remaining water and boil for 1 minute, then add mixture to the milk. Mix well.
4. Add brandy, then beat mixture with egg beater for 2 minutes.
5. Serve in large mugs.

Cranberry Glogg

6 cups cranberry juice cocktail
6 whole cloves
2 cinnamon sticks
cinnamon schnapps to taste

1. Combine juice, cloves, and cinnamon in a large saucepan.
2. Warm over a medium heat for 15 minutes. Reduce heat and let sit for 5 minutes.
3. Remove cinnamon sticks and cloves.
4. Pour into mugs.
5. Add schnapps as desired, depending on the amount of warmth you have in mind.

Christmas Irish Cream

1 can (12-ounce) sweetened condensed milk
8 ounces Irish whiskey
4 large eggs
1 tablespoon chocolate syrup
1 teaspoon vanilla extract
1 teaspoon coconut extract

1. Mix all ingredients together in a blender.
2. Chill for 1 hour before serving.

Coffee Liqueur for Christmas

4 cups granulated sugar
2 ounces instant coffee crystals
2 cups water
3 cups vodka
1 vanilla bean, split in half lengthwise

1. Mix sugar and coffee in the bottom of a large pitcher.
2. Add water.
3. Chill for 90 minutes; then add vodka. Mix well.
4. Drop the vanilla bean into an empty half-gallon
   bottle with a screw top.
5. Pour the coffee mixture into the bottle, seal, and
   store for 30 days in a dark place.

Hot Candy Cane in a Holiday Mug

two cups hot cocoa

peppermint liqueur

whipped cream

two red maraschino
   cherries, halved

two green maraschino cherries, halved

1. Pour hot cocoa into 2 large mugs.
2. Add peppermint liqueur to taste.
3. Top with whipped cream and red and
   green cherries.

Note: Cocoa made from scratch is best, but
   prepared mixes to which you add boiling
   water will serve, too.

Hot Cinnamon Stocking

two cups hot cocoa
cinnamon-flavored liqueur
whipped cream
two red maraschino cherries, halved
two green maraschino cherries, halved

1. Pour hot cocoa into 2 large mugs.
2. Add cinnamon-flavored liqueur to taste.
3. Top with whipped cream and red and
   green cherries.

Note: Cocoa made from scratch is best, but
prepared mixes to which you add boiling
water will serve, too.

Hot Spiced Cider

Servings: 4

1 teaspoon whole cloves

$\frac{1}{4}$ teaspoon nutmeg

dash ginger

1 quart cider, fresh pressed if available

5 cinnamon sticks

4 thin orange slices

1. Place the cloves, nutmeg, and ginger in a tea ball.
2. Pour the cider into a large saucepan into which one of the cinnamon sticks has been placed. Hang the tea ball on the side of the pot, being sure that it is submerged in the cider.
3. Float the orange slices on top. Heat to a temperature just below a simmer, and allow cider to cook for at least 15 minutes.
4. To serve, place one cinnamon stick in each of four mugs and pour cider in, leaving the oranges and cinnamon stick in the pot. (Careful—it will be hot!)
5. If desired, one jigger of bourbon can be added to each mug.

Irish Coffee

Servings: 1

1 jigger Irish whiskey
1 teaspoon sugar
1 cup very hot after-dinner coffee
2 tablespoons whipped cream

1. Pour the whiskey into a heatproof glass or mug.
2. Stir in the sugar and add the hot coffee.
3. Top with whipped cream and serve immediately.

Perfect Egg Nog

6 large eggs, separated
$\frac{1}{2}$ cup granulated sugar
1 pint heavy cream
1 pint milk
1 pint whiskey
2 ounces rum

1. Place eggs in a large bowl.
2. Add sugar to the yolks, beating at medium speed.
3. Beat egg whites until very stiff; mix them with the yolk mixture.
4. Stir in the cream and milk.
5. Add whiskey and rum. Stir thoroughly.
6. Chill for 2 hours. Serve with grated nutmeg on top.

Wassail

2 quarts apple cider
2 cups orange juice
1 cup fresh lemon juice
1 teaspoon cloves
cinnamon sticks

1. Put apple cider, orange juice, and lemon juice into a large saucepan. Add the cloves and two cinnamon sticks. Warm over medium heat for 20 minutes.
2. When ready to serve, strain to remove cloves and cinnamon sticks, and pour liquid into mugs.
3. Place a new cinnamon stick in each mug and serve.

Note: A teaspoon of honey may be substituted for the cloves.